# Witham &
# District

## IN OLD PHOTOGRAPHS

### JOHN PALOMBI

Sutton Publishing Limited
Phoenix Mill · Thrupp · Stroud
Gloucestershire · GL5 2BU

*Witham and Countryside Society*

First Published 1995

Reprinted 2004

Copyright © John Palombi, 1995

*Cover photograph: Colchester Road, Witham.*

**British Library Cataloguing in Publication Data.**
A catalogue record for this book is available from
the British Library.

ISBN 0-7509-0847-5

Typeset in 9/10 Sabon.
Typesetting and origination by
Sutton Publishing Limited.
Printed and bound in England by
J.H. Haynes & Co. Ltd, Sparkford.

Lockram Lane is an old road, now a footpath, whose curve follows the 'half-acres' from the Newland Street junction with Collingwood Road down to the mill in Guithavon Valley. The cottages, which were demolished to make way for a car park, probably began life as weavers' cottages, hence the name 'Lockram' which was a type of baize. The lane was once known as Queen Street and, before that, Church Lane.

# *Contents*

Dorothy L. Sayers was a novelist and Dante scholar, who lived and worked in Witham from 1940 until her death in 1957. She was author of the Peter Wimsey detective novels, the radio series *Man born to be King* and a translation of Dante. She was a well-known figure in the town and is shown here in wartime dress! A statue of her now stands almost opposite her home in Newland Street.

# *Introduction*

To fully appreciate this collection of photographs it may be useful to consider the history of Witham and its development over the last thousand years. The first record was in AD 912 with the building of an earthwork fortification to repel the Danes. This was known as a 'burh', and survives as the low hill around the railway station. In this Saxon period Essex was divided into administrative areas called 'hundreds', each with a court for dealing with thieves, collecting taxes and recording the owners of estates. These 'moots' were held monthly and one was at Witham. The place now considered most likely as its site is outside the burh between the Chipping Hill Green and the river, now known as Moat Farm. The town of Witham grew around it and this area became known as 'Chipping Hill' from the Saxon for 'the hill of the market'.

In 1147 the Royal Manor of Witham was granted to the Knights Templar, a powerful order of 'monks in arms' whose wealth and influence spread right across Europe to the Holy Land. Half a century later they saw the opportunity of establishing a market on the old Roman road that passed through the manor and in 1212 they founded a 'new town'. King John granted a charter for a weekly market here and an annual fair. Houses and shops were built on both sides of the road that widened as it led up the gravel slope from the river crossing. Each tenant had a narrow strip of land with a standard frontage to Newland Street, known as a 'half-acre', and the new Witham was born.

The Knights Templar's new town was probably limited initially to the area between Mill Lane and Avenue Road. One reason it prospered could be because Witham is only 6 miles from Maldon, then the most important town in Essex after Colchester. The little market town continued to grow and soon became a centre for the cloth trade. Memories of that trade live on with street names such as Lockram Lane (lockram was a form of baize).

In the eighteenth century Witham became a fashionable town. Coaches from Norwich and Ipswich passed through as Witham was the first overnight stop on journeys from London. This included the journey to Harwich for travellers to Holland and Germany. By 1836, just before the coming of the railway, there were twenty licensed stage-coaches operating between Chelmsford and Colchester.

In this period many new buildings were added to Newland Street and older buildings were given a brick front to keep in with the smart new trend. These brick embellishments were only a façade, as the original timber-framed buildings were retained behind. In many instances false windows were built into the façades purely for the sake of appearances, especially where the brick front exceeded the height of the original building. These false windows can still be seen in Newland Street buildings, many of which have survived to the present day. This was the last period of great change in Newland Street, as the photographs in this book demonstrate; the appearance of the central part of the town has changed little in the last hundred years.

By this time Chipping Hill had become a backwater mainly occupied by labourers. For this reason the smart new brick façades were much less evident, and other forms of development also bypassed the area. The medieval character of the original village remains, and the photographs in this book show how little this small community has changed.

The coming of the railways had a major impact, with the Eastern Counties Railway opening their line from Colchester to London in 1843. This brought London to within two hours by train. Branches to Maldon and Braintree opened in 1848. To begin with coach operators loaded their coaches on to railway wagons for much of their journey, but some unfortunate and serious accidents brought this practice to an abrupt halt. Witham itself experienced a railway disaster in 1905 when the Cromer express left the rails outside the station. Postcards of this event were soon on sale but not, understandably, on railway premises! Three examples are included in this book.

As the coaching trade rapidly declined, with the cloth trade already gone, Witham had to rely on other industries. The good agricultural land surrounding the town had provided a sound milling and malting industry for many years and this expanded with the mills in Guithavon Valley and Chipping Hill investing in steam engines to supplement time-honoured water power. The maltings by the railway station was established in 1874, continuing the malting traditions of the town, and the area became known for its seed industry. The firm of Cooper Taber originated in 1887 and in 1961 merged with other leading seed houses to form Hurst Gunson and Cooper Taber. Cullens Seeds was established in

Chipping Hill in the 1870s, and by 1900 trade had expanded across the country and as far as Europe and the United States of America. The firm of Crittalls came to the town in 1919 and was manufacturing metal windows there by 1927. Chipping Hill also had a glove factory from 1912 to 1966.

It was during this period of industrial renewal that photography became established, and the town has been fortunate with the record of the expansion and changes that this particular medium achieved. The stationers on the corner of Guithavon Street (there has been one there for over a hundred years) produced postcards recording these changes, many of which have survived to the present day. A number of photographers have worked in the town over that period including Fred Spalding of Chelmsford and Fred Hayward of Witham, both of whom produced many postcards.

This book has of course relied heavily on the postcards produced over the last one hundred years (it was on 1 September 1894 that the Post Office decreed that privately and commercially published cards could be sent through the post). This has provided the reader with a visual record of the development of the town, its celebrations, its disasters and the lifestyle of its residents. These have been supplemented by the albums and collections of the town's residents which have been kindly made available for this book. It has therefore been possible to assemble many previously unpublished photographs to provide a more personal record of the expansion and prosperity of the town since the 1860s.

The greatest and most rapid expansion of Witham came in the 1960s when the town was developed to provide for a Greater London 'overspill'. A large industrial estate was established and much of the town's surrounding farmland was built over to provide land for new housing. This photographic record covers a time from the small market town of the end of the last century to the modern town of rapid change in the 1960s.

The surrounding villages which have long-established ties with Witham have been included to provide a broader view of town and countryside life over the last century. Silver End was built by Crittalls for their workforce, Rivenhall and Hatfield Peverel sit either side of the town on the London to Colchester trunk road. Wickham Bishops, White Notley, Terling and Faulkbourne nestle around the town in a more rural environment. It is hoped that this collection of photographs gives an insight into the life and times of Witham and the surrounding countryside over the last century and more.

# SECTION ONE

# Newland Street: Around the Town Centre

This is an insight into early nineteenth-century Witham. In 1836 there were twenty coaches daily between Chelmsford and Colchester calling at Witham inns. Witham was six hours from London, and the first overnight stop.

This aerial view of the town was taken in 1920 when there were still green fields between Newland Street and the railway station. The view demonstrates how the town clustered around the Roman road, with very limited expansion until well into this century.

Newland Street from a similar viewpoint to the print on page 8. The large house on the extreme right, Avenue House, was owned by the Du-cane family and used as the dower house of The Grove (see pp. 52–4), and the terrace further down housed the butler.

THE MANSE, WITHAM.
BY F.H.

Newbury House, adjacent to Avenue House above, was the manse of the Congregational church from 1832 to 1934. The minister living there was killed by the accidental explosion of a hand-grenade in 1916.

This study of Dorothy L. Sayers shows her at work, possibly in the room on the first floor of 24 Newland Street where she did all of her writing.

Dorothy L. Sayers' house was part of the group of three cottages with the two ornamental yews outside. High House, behind the wall on the left, was later reduced to two storeys some time after this picture was taken, probably early this century.

No. 18 Newland Street, known as Whitehall, was the residence of a prominent lawyer from 1840 to the First World War, when it became an army billet. It was Witham College, as in this picture, from 1919 to 1925.

Whitehall was then purchased for use as a cinema, which was financed by selling the extensive grounds, and opened in 1927. Changing times forced closure in 1964 and Essex CC acquired it in 1971. It was eventually converted to a library which opened in November 1981.

Towards Colchester, just after the turn of the century. The Red Lion, on the right, was a downmarket lodging house in the eighteenth century and advertised cock-fights. Green's was a grocery shop which also stocked bulbs and seeds.

Towards Colchester on the other side of the road. Dorothy L. Sayers' cottage may be seen on the left, with the ornamental yews outside. This was before the terrace next to the George was converted to shops.

This view, in the early 1950s, shows the Red Lion with its timbers exposed and the vehicles and street furniture of the period.

A rear view of High House from the back garden where Miss Cook is tending the flowers. The top storey of this building was removed, making the name less appropriate and spoiling the proportions of the building. It is now a Chinese restaurant.

This fine view of Newland Street was taken with a panoramic camera, which swivelled on a pivot. It was published by Afford's of Newland Street as a 'panoramicard'. The George, on the left, has been a public house since about 1807. Collingwood Road was built to connect the high street with the railway station in about 1872, and the George

was restructured with a new brick gable to facilitate road widening at that time. On the right of the picture is Blythe's flour mills shop. Blythe had the mill in Guithavon Valley and sold 'corn, bird seeds, linseed and cotton cakes, Spratt's patent dog biscuits and general forage'.

This view of Newland Street shows the row of shops demolished in order to build Newlands shopping precinct in the 1960s. W. Reed, the ironmonger, is on the corner, which dates the picture to before 1905.

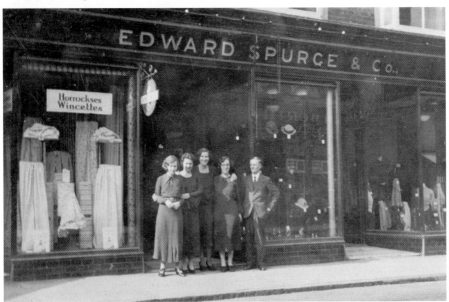

The second shop down on the right is Spurge's grocer's and draper's business. It lasted from around 1890 through to the time the buildings were demolished in the 1960s. This is the shop staff of 1935.

Also in the same row is William Gage's hairdresser's and tobacconist, seen here in 1906. Billy Clarke worked here as a hairdresser from 1906 until 1936, when he opened his own shop in Maldon Road. He continued until his retirement at the age of ninety-one.

This is the attractive Georgian shop front for a cabinet-maker, upholsterer and antique business. The shop was demolished to make way for a new Tesco store, which has now given place to the entrance to the Grove Centre.

Newlands shopping precinct was built in the 1960s mainly on the grounds of a large house called The Wilderness. This view of the house, before the ground floor was converted to shops, dates from around the turn of the century. The house faced down Maldon Road.

By the mid-1960s times were changing, Witham was expanding rapidly and a new shopping precinct was the order of the day. This photograph shows The Wilderness boarded and demolition in progress.

Taken soon after the last picture, this is a view of the site after demolition of The Wilderness. Budgen was still trading until it, in turn, was demolished.

The White Hart became the most important of the coaching inns of Witham, and was a meeting place of the Essex Hunt. Dating from the fifteenth century it was extended in the sixteenth century.

The Angel stood on the opposite corner of Maldon Road to the White Hart. It was demolished in 1927 to make way for a wider road to Maldon, and was replaced by Central Buildings. The corner of the White Hart was remodelled at the same time.

This shows The Wilderness together with other shops in their final state, before redevelopment, in the 1950s. Turning at the lights is a Blythe's lorry, from the mill in Guithavon Valley.

The International Stores occupied premises between Maldon Road and the Spread Eagle from about 1898 to the 1970s. This picture shows the shop staff probably before the First World War.

Maldon Road, about 1900. The then Baptist chapel on the right has long since ceased to be used for religious purposes and is currently vacant.

A little further down Maldon Road at about the same time. The cottages on the left have been replaced by a wine bar. The road was then known as Maldon Lane and had a much more rural feel to it.

Jack Hollick was born on Christmas Day, 1905. He started stitching shoes in the garden shed in his spare time for additional income. He then rented a tiny shop in Newland Street until he had his own shop built in Maldon Road.

Jack Hollick and his wife in their premises in Maldon Road. They were married in 1935, and had a boy and a girl. Their son John still runs the family business.

Another view of Maldon Road with Mr Brewster, the saddler, outside his shop on the right. Further down on the left is the Bell public house and Maldon Road School.

This view looks back towards Newland Street. Maldon Road School (now a youth centre) and the Bell are clearly visible. The school was erected in 1837 and enlarged in 1894. At this time, about 1917, the master was Ernest Quick.

This closer view of the Bell gives a good idea of life around the First World War. Public health concerning food and drink establishments has always been a problem. James Harvey was ordered to remove pigsties from the Bell yard by the Inspector of the Board of Health on 7 August 1852.

Newland Street frontages have changed very little over the past two hundred years or so. This engraving views the town from approximately where the market cross once stood. The date is pre-1840 as space between buildings on the left had not yet been widened to form Guithavon Street.

On the corner of Guithavon Street on Witham's Red Cross day, 1917. There has been a stationer here for well over a hundred years.

Looking down Newland Street from Guithavon Street about the turn of the century.
Afford, the stationers on the corner at that time, was also a photographer and published
many postcards from then to around 1920.

Guithavon Street, built about 1840, soon contained private residences. This pleasant
garden preceded the Barclays Business Centre, and the house is now a food take-away.
Judging by the dress, this photograph was probably taken around the Second World
War.

Newland Street's market and annual fair were chartered in 1212. By 1870, when this photograph was taken, itinerant traders and the pleasure element had brought the fair into disrepute; this was the last recorded event.

This picture is inscribed as 'the town band playing the dead march and hymns' on 20 May 1910. The crowd had gathered outside Witham House (now the Midland Bank), a common event on important occasions before the war.

Sammy Page ran a second-hand business in Newland Street from about 1910 to the 1940s. It was in the shop which now sells cake decorating materials. He is pictured outside his shop in 1924 with his younger daughter Elizabeth.

The Batsford Court, now a hotel, was the premises of 'Chartered Surveyors, Auctioneers and Valuers' Balch & Balch from the early 1920s to the late 1970s. 'Battesford' was one of the ancient manors of Witham.

The earliest post to Witham was from London and cost 3*d*. By 1811 it was 6*d*, and then came William Hill's penny post of 1840. Parcel post did not start until 1883, and C. Webster of Whitechapel (shown above) arrived at Witham at 3.15 a.m. and returned to London at 11.15 p.m.

Witham post office and staff, September 1910. This post office at Medina Villas (now Coopers) lasted until 1939 when the new post office at the other end of Newland Street opened. This closed in 1994.

Newland Street with military manoeuvres around the First World War. The post office may be seen on the right with most buildings still recognizable.

Further down is the Crotchet, which was the tap room of the Blue Posts Inn. This major coaching inn did not survive the demise of the coaching trade after the railways came. Next to it was the old forge, seen here at the turn of the century. It has now made way for a bar extension.

On the same side of the road was an open space (since developed for sheltered housing) used for caravan sales until 1980. This promotional shot dates from around 1960.

Newland Street at the turn of the century looking back to the town centre. On the left is the old Constitutional Club. The town clock is on the wall with its bell turret on the roof. The bell was returned to St Nicolas' Church after the building burned down.

The General Election of January 1910 and
Sir Fortescue Flannery, the Conservative
party candidate, poses for the camera.
Feelings ran high at election time and at
the previous election Afford's, the
stationers along the street, printed leaflets
for the Liberal candidate which so
offended the Conservative supporters that
they closed their accounts with him.

A view of the Constitutional Club during
that 1910 election campaign, with party
workers posing outside.

The United Reform church (formerly Congregational) was built in 1840, replacing the 'dear old patched up meeting house' of 1715. It was originally hidden from Newland Street by the Constitutional Club which stood in front until it burned down in 1910.

This is probably the crew and engine that attended the fire. The basket attached to the rear of the engine was used to prevent the hose clogging when water was pumped from a pond.

The Constitutional Club caught fire on 10 February 1910. The fire brigade had to round up the horses in a field in Guithavon Street, then harness them, so by the time they got to the building it was well alight and soon burned down. The building was used as a Literary Institute where the town's entertainment took place, such as penny readings and musical evenings. It was eventually replaced by a new club in Collingwood Road.

Newland Street looking east in the 1930s. Lloyds Bank is still there, but a new NatWest Bank is now next door. The buildings that remain are remarkably unchanged.

The same buildings, this time looking south, in the 1950s. Again, notwithstanding changed occupation, the only new building is the NatWest Bank, which replaced the 'Newlands Café'.

No. 83 Newland Street, when it was Palmer's bakery. Edward Palmer ran the business, with a bakery at the rear, until the Second World War. The property continued as a bakery until it closed in the late 1980s, and has remained empty since.

This bunting could be to celebrate the end of the First World War, when Fern House (on the right) was even then the doctor's surgery, and the building on the left (now a pharmacy) was then a school.

Witham's first Co-op was at 85 Newland Street, before moving to the new premises a little further down the street. The building had previously housed the post office, which moved across the road in 1887.

Horse-drawn vehicles ready to start delivery rounds for Witham Co-op. This shop had two elegant lamps over the shop windows. Later the Co-op expanded into the adjacent Pelican House, bearing the pelican crest of the Pattison family who once owned the building.

The bottom of Newland Street, showing the gasworks house on the corner of Mill Lane. On the right is the Crotchet, next to what was once the Blue Posts Inn.

This view, from the Mill Lane junction looking towards the town centre, shows the original Glover's building, now a vacant site, and the Globe, which is now a glaziers.

The same time and place, but looking in the opposite direction. Bridge Street has lost many of the buildings on the left foreground of this picture, but further back much of the property remains.

A fine etching of 23–27 Bridge Street, probably early in the last century. The buildings remain substantially unchanged although the Morning Star, on the left, has been demolished and rebuilt further back. The George & Dragon, just the other side, is now residential accommodation.

It was agreed in 1834, at a meeting in the Blue Posts Inn, to establish a gasworks in the town on the corner of Mill Lane (seen here in the centre background) at a cost of £850. The primary purpose was for street lighting, and the gasworks ceased production in 1950.

Another £850 was spent in 1847 to provide a new gasometer and extend the pipes to the station and Chipping Hill. This picture was taken considerably later, when further extensions were made.

Bridge Street, a little further south, probably before the First World War. Motive power had changed as well as increased, but the buildings remain noticeably unaltered.

Robert Fleuty took over his father's wheelwright business in Howbridge Road in 1874. The wheelwright was an essential trade in the town when horses were so important to the local economy. The motor trade has now taken over this role.

George Armond bequeathed rent from the Spread Eagle in Newland Street for the provision of almshouses for poor widows. This picture of the junction of Bridge Street and Spinks Lane shows the almshouses on the left. Mr Fleuty is standing on the corner about to gather some compost for his garden.

The almshouses, pictured here just before demolition in the 1960s, were built in 1507 and conveyed to the trustees of ten widows in 1687, when relocated from near to The Grove.

# SECTION TWO

# Expansion with Prosperity

The parish church at Chipping Hill had become overcrowded, and a chapel of ease was built on land, which became Guithavon Street, donated by Mr W.H. Pattison. The church was consecrated on 1 November 1842 and this print dates from that time.

Times and habits change. By 1969 the church was closed but reopened in 1989 after major refurbishment by the Roman Catholic community. The interior has changed significantly from its original state shown here.

A church school was built next to the church (seen to the right of the church in the print opposite). The school was demolished to provide a car park in the late 1960s.

These two photographs show both infants' classes of about 1920, in a typical classroom of that period.

Witham Police Station in Guithavon Street which, when the new station in Colchester Road was opened in 1937, became the first base for the Essex Police Driver Training School. The building was demolished in the 1980s and sheltered housing now occupies the site.

Witham division of the Essex Constabulary, 1892; a fine collection of the law enforcers of the last century. The officer in charge was Superintendent Allen.

Special Constables of Rivenhall and Little Braxted, 1914–17. Some familiar names associated with Witham include: A.W. Shelly, J. Cullen, W. Chanmer, Revd H.H. Willmott, W. Brice, W. & J. Taber.

War Reserve Constables at Witham Police Station in 1944. Wally West, on the extreme left, was employed there as gardener/handyman for many years. He still cycled almost daily from Rivenhall to Witham when well into his eighties.

Witham Home Guard, 1943. Meetings were held at the Church House on Sunday mornings and the Albert Yard was often used as the drill ground.

The Mill House in Guithavon Valley. Mr E.M. Blythe, miller and corn merchant, had owned the mill for twenty years before replacing the millstones with 'modern' roller mills in about 1890. This may well have been his wife photographed at the rear of the house at about that time.

A river view, near Witham, late in the last century. A cart, reminiscent of Constable's *Haywain*, is soaking its wheels in the river to seal them tightly against the metal tyres.

Guithavon Road was built jointly by Hoffgard Shoobridge, miller until the 1870s, and J. Pattison of Witham House. Shoobridge built the Highfields Road end (from the bend seen in this view) and Pattison the Mill Lane access. It has changed very little since this First World War photograph.

The Grove was a large house situated behind the substantial wall opposite the war memorial in Newland Street. It was built in 1696 by Robert Barwell and enlarged in 1720 by Earl Abercorn, who built the existing wall.

In 1761 Princess Charlotte stayed at The Grove on her way from Germany to marry George III. One can imagine her descending this staircase as she left after breakfast to arrive at St James's Palace for her wedding at about 3 p.m.

The house was lavishly furnished, including mahogany doors with Adam surrounds and some fine panelling. This dining-room measured 24 ft by 20 ft and had a fireplace with a white marble mantel and hearth with Lincrusta dado and ceiling. This photograph is from the sale catalogue of 1921.

The Grove cottages in Newland Street were built for the gardeners. This catalogue photograph includes the trough used by the town water-cart to reduce dust from the roads during dry weather.

The Avenue was originally planted by Earl Abercorn for visual effect, and made into a carriageway by Percy Lawrence in the nineteenth century. A lodge and gates were erected at the station end and the lodge and one gatepost have survived to the 1990s.

The Avenue was planted with lime trees and this view, showing a First World War mounted soldier, looks down from the lodge towards The Grove.

This carriageway still had to cross the main road. The Newland Street end had only railings to protect it. The traffic along the Colchester Road was busy even in Mr Lawrence's time and he complained that his garden was covered in grey dust during dry weather.

The limes were felled to provide building land after the house was demolished and the Grove properties sold. This 1930s view of The Avenue shows the road before it was finished.

Percy Lawrence died in 1921 and his executors sold the house to Charles Bentall. However, almost immediately his business fell on hard times and the house was soon empty and on the market again. Many looked at it, including Winston Churchill, but it was not sold and the fittings were disposed of by auction and the building demolished in 1932. This picture shows the house just as demolition had begun.

The demolition crew who carried out the job.

Some fittings were saved from the original house and used in the conversion of the stables to another, smaller, house. This photograph was taken before it mysteriously burned down in 1967.

The gardens were once described by Daniel Defoe (referring to Earl Abercorn's son): 'His lordship is finishing his gardens in such a manner as few in that part of England will exceed them.' This picture shows a Red Cross demonstration in 1953 at the rear of the later house.

The Essex Agricultural Show was held in Witham in 1863 and 1910. This view of the 1910 Show illustrates the entrance from Collingwood Road. The show was held in the fields either side of The Avenue.

Visitors to the 1910 Show are seen here walking to the entrance at the other end of The Avenue opposite The Grove.

Avenue Road in the 1920s, before development of the south side. In the background is one of the buildings relating to the cattle market, which stood on the site now occupied by the Labour party constituency offices.

The other end of Avenue Road, showing the old Catholic church which was opened in 1851 by Cardinal Wiseman. It then served an area stretching from Burnham-on-Crouch to Dunmow. The church closed when the refurbished All Saints' Church was opened in 1989.

Blunts Hall was one of the ancient manors of Witham. The house dates from the thirteenth century, but has had many alterations and additions since. It is pictured here earlier this century.

The labourers of Blunts Hall Farm at about the same time.

Witham Lodge was a large house which burned down in mysterious circumstances in the late 1960s. The Witham Lodge Estate now occupies the site.

The YMCA showing the 'Boss Lady', believed to be Mrs Round of Chipping Hill, about 1920. The hut was a First World War army hut which was later used by the Royal British Legion before their premises in Newland Street were built in the early 1950s. The hut is now occupied by a second-hand dealer.

Collingwood Road in the 1920s, showing the water-tower which was built in 1868 and demolished in 1936. The Public Hall, Pelican Cottage, Bygrove and Collingwood House are also featured.

Langleys, a fine six-bedroom redbrick house, was built in 1917 and occupied by the Mens family until acquired for development by Witham Urban District Council in 1959. It was demolished in 1976 to make way for the present Area Health Authority offices.

A portrait of Mrs Mens in the porch of Langleys, about 1920. The demolition of this house was just one of many controversial developments in the late 1960s and early 1970s in Witham.

The back garden of Langleys, about the same time, showing the Collingwood Road water-tower in the background.

Collingwood Road was built in 1872 to provide a road between Newland Street and the railway station. Once completed, development of property began and the Public Hall was opened by Lord Rayleigh on Easter Monday, 1894. This photograph was taken in the late 1920s.

When the Constitutional Club in Newland Street burned down in 1910, it was replaced by this building next to the Public Hall. This photograph was taken soon after it was built.

The Jubilee Oak stands at the junction of Collingwood Road and Guithavon Valley. It was planted by Lady Luard on 8 December 1887 to commemorate the Golden Jubilee of Queen Victoria. This photograph was taken in 1900.

The Witham Nursing Home, photographed in 1930, was built ten years earlier by voluntary subscription. It must have seen the birth of hundreds of Witham babies. It closed when Sister M. Glassfield retired in 1955, as it was no longer considered economical to staff a two-bedroom hospital.

Boy Scouts marching past the Jubilee Oak to a memorial service on 20 May 1910. Church House, seen in the background, was built in 1909.

The wedding party of Albert George Bright (aged twenty-two) and Mabel Mary Chalk (aged twenty-one) on the steps of Church House. The wedding took place at St Nicolas' Church on 5 April 1920.

The original narrow metal bridge, which carried Collingwood Road over the railway line at the station, was replaced with a wider brick and concrete structure in the late 1960s. This photograph was taken as work began, and shows one of the cattle market buildings on the extreme left.

The junction of Rickstones Road and Cressing Road, about 1930. The buildings visible in the photograph still survive, although since changed, and are now joined by some later in-filling.

The Cherry Tree public house in Cressing Road with two wagons and their teams of horses. The blind window, which was used to advertise the name of the inn above the front door, still survives to identify the building.

The Victoria public house at Powers Hall End, around 1920. The building is still recognizable, although the rural aspect of the yard has changed dramatically since that time.

# SECTION THREE

# Business and Pleasure

These three properties were prominent Witham buildings in the early part of this century. The building in the middle was Miss Hunt's residential school. It was demolished in 1939 and a new Barclays Bank was built on the site. The bank had previously occupied the building on the right (now the Town Hall).

Cricket has been played in Witham since 1820. The club moved to Guithavon Street in 1840, and then to the grounds at the rear of Witham House (the third building above).

Witham Football Team, 1902–3. The football club also played in the recreation grounds at the rear of Witham House (now the Midland Bank) before moving to their present ground in the 1970s.

In 1946 the park was leased to Crittalls who maintained it and let it to any club who wished to use it. This is the Witham Horse Show of 1949.

Witham Co-op children's day, also in the recreation grounds. There is no date for this photograph, but the dress suggests it would be about 1920.

A view of the recreation ground in 1905, five years after it was officially opened on 20 June 1900. It was owned by Percy Lawrence of the Grove, who gave it to the town 'in perpetuity' in 1903.

Two water-tanks, at the former waterworks behind the Swan in Newland Street, were converted into a swimming bath and opened on 27 May 1933 by Sir Valentine Crittall. This may well have been the opening ceremony, as Sir Valentine is shown seated with several members of Witham Council.

The pavilion of Witham Bowls Club in the early 1950s, with Gus Goodey, Ian MacBeth and Kath Richards (who later became leader of Braintree District Council).

Glover's cycle shop in Newland Street opposite Mill Lane, about 1900. He had started an interest in the automobile even then, with an 1898/9 Benz (left) and a Daimler parked outside.

Glover Bros Witham Motor & Cycle Works on the corner of Collingwood Road where they traded until the late 1930s. This photograph was taken much earlier, probably before 1920.

For a time Glover's Garage was adjacent to the bridge. Mr Glover, wearing a buttonhole, poses in front of about seventy cars for the wedding of Mr Duncan Rowe and Miss Francis Mary Allen in July 1913. This building was one of the first purpose-built public garages and workshops in the country. Ginetta cars were built here from the 1950s to the late 1980s.

The last Glover's Garage, on the corner of The Avenue, in the early 1960s.

The Grove Service Station, on the corner of Avenue Road, in 1952. This has since been developed, but is still a car sales and service station. It was owned by Hurrell and Beardwell until the 1980s.

Hurrell and Beardwell started in White Horse Lane, Chipping Hill, in the early 1920s, and this photograph was probably taken in the 1930s. A house-building company's offices now occupy the site.

The 1960 Witham Carnival, with Austin Beardwell driving the leading car, a 1934 Austin Seven. It is followed by the 1960 version soon to be known simply as the Mini, driven by Cyril Simmonds.

The first Witham Hospital Carnival was held in 1926. The Queen was Pat Jones of the Spread Eagle and the King was Ron Briggs of Collingwood Road. The Royal Justice was the Rt. Hon. E.W. Sharp.

The staff of Witham station, when it was known as Witham Junction. The date is early this century, but unfortunately was not recorded for this photograph.

On Friday 1 September 1905 the 9.27 a.m. fast train from Liverpool Street was derailed entering Witham station, killing ten passengers and injuring many more. Several of the train's fourteen carriages were scattered across the lines like the one shown above.

The fifth carriage turned at right angles, fell on its side and rolled over completely with wheels uppermost. The great weight of the undercarriage caused it to collapse like a crushed eggshell. Most of the dead were in this carriage.

The original entrance to Witham station was in Easton Road and only a footbridge, seen in this view of the disaster, accessed Albert Road. The booking office was built on the bridge in 1907.

This view of a train preparing to leave for Maldon East on 29 June 1957 typifies an Anglian country station with a rural branch-line train just after the Second World War. The engine is class J15 0–6–0 No. 65468.

The station water-tower and unusual signal-box overhanging the Braintree branch in the 1950s. The British Railways standard class 7MT No. 70008 'Black Prince' was a common sight on Anglian main-line trains at that time.

Seen passing through the station from London is a typical pre-nationalization Liverpool Street to Norwich train, in this case a class B12/3 4–6–0 No. 1542.

Colchester end of Witham station in the late 1950s. The original station maltings can be seen clearly on the right before Hugh Baird & Sons redeveloped and modernized their maltings, from 1962.

The Crittalls Witham factory from the air, about 1965. The expansion of Witham has just begun with the first factories being built on what will become the town's industrial estate. Bellfield Road is yet to be built.

The frontage of the same factory, also about 1965. The factory was built in 1919 as a sheet-metal factory but the metal window business was moved here in 1927, and a galvanizing plant added in 1939.

The auxiliary fire-pump tender and crew for the Crittalls factory between 1935 and 1945 when production changed to armaments. Despite this, the Witham factory survived the Second World War, but not the changing world of the 1990s. Demolished in 1993 after the work was transferred to a new factory in Braintree, a superstore now occupies the site.

This Cooper Taber Ltd building, pictured here new, lasted less than thirty years before it was demolished to make way for a new office development.

The major expansion of Witham in the late 1960s and early 1970s was mainly on farmland. The houses surrounding Highfields Road were built on what was Highfields Farm. This picture of the farmhouse, which was situated on the left of Highfields Road going up towards Chipping Hill, was taken in the 1960s just before its demolition.

Another farm, close to the centre of Witham, which has now disappeared without trace was Cock's Farm at Chipping Hill. The farmhouse, pictured here, was sited in Braintree Road near the railway bridge.

Most of the Forest Road Estate was built on Half Hides Farm land. This photograph of the soon to be demolished farmhouse, again in the 1960s, shows the rural areas close to Witham before the 'overspill' developments.

William Pinkham married Rebecca Fowler in 1884 when he was twenty-two and she twenty. They started their own glove-making business in Torrington, Devon, and in 1901 the family moved to Witham. He was employed as a political agent and in his spare time continued to make gloves in their house in Albert Road. By 1904 several girls were employed and two more houses nearby were taken over. This photograph was taken inside the factory built in 1912 next to the railway bridge.

This is the first factory, which was built in 1912 in Chipping Hill. More factories were added until the advent of the world slump, and the company folded in 1927.

The business restarted and by 1948 Pinkham's had three hundred indoor workers and a similar number of outworkers producing around 4,000 dozen pairs of gloves a week. These are some of the indoor workers of the Witham factory in 1947/8.

W.H. Leslie Pinkham, son of William Pinkham, in 1960. He took over the running of the business on his father's death in 1938. Foreign competition, together with fashion turning away from gloves in the 1960s, led to a decline in trade and Pinkhams went out of business in 1966. The building was demolished in the 1980s and today a small development of flats occupies the site.

# Chipping Hill, the Original Settlement

'A Roman station at Chipping Hill'. This engraving of 1832 depicts the River Brain looking towards St Nicolas' Church and Moat Farm. The stile is on the path from Shoobridge's Mill to Moat Farm, between the river and the burh.

Chipping Hill from the air no later than the mid-1920s. The access to the church was then by a track next to the houses on the green.

Until 1971 Chipping Hill gently curved from the station bridge down to the forge. This view, from a postcard dated 1906, shows the Albert on the extreme right and Temple Villas in the middle distance. A house called Temples, which was demolished to make way for Bellfield Road in 1970, may be seen between them.

The Albert in the 1960s. The figurehead, displayed outside until 1993, is seen here in all its glory.

This is a very early engraving of the forge predating photography. The building dates from 1375 and has been a smithy for at least four hundred years. Horses are no longer shod here but the forge continues its ironwork business.

A busier view around the turn of the century showing children outside Barnardiston House, then a private school. The house was bought for £100 in 1630 by Lady Catherine Barnardiston who endowed it for charitable purposes. It has been a nursing home since 1984.

This postcard view, dated 1927, looks across to Chipping Hill from near the station bridge. Earlsmead, on the extreme right, was demolished to make way for the new turning of that name, and Moat Farm, including the original farmhouse and farm buildings, is in the left background.

The White Horse public house has changed little from the outside for many years. This photograph of 1930 shows the publican at that time, Cyril Rollings, with his wife Irene and son Billy.

Two more of Afford's 'panoramicards'. These views of Chipping Hill date between 1900 and 1920. The cottages on the green, at the centre of this view, were demolished

The five-way junction at Chipping Hill. Here the track from Newland Street met the roads to Braintree (via Faulkbourne), Colchester (via Rivenhall) and Cressing (Church Street).

in 1935. The workmen got a bonus to clear them and the rubble in time for an important wedding.

In this photograph the cottages on the left contained John Baron's sweet shop in the 1920s and 1930s. The shop closed in 1936 and the row was demolished soon after. A chalet bungalow now occupies the site.

A little further along was the old post office and store. It was run by the Doole family from the 1890s to the 1940s. The cottages this side of the old shop were demolished to make way for Chauntry Villas in 1897.

An evening vista from the church tower. Moat Farm, demolished in the 1950s, can be seen with the fields across the river where the Moat Farm housing estate now stands.

The old Manor House, an important building standing on the south side of the green, was probably never a manor house. The nineteenth-century shop, seen on the extreme right, was a cobbler's shop which doubled as a dairy farm shop before the war. The business finally closed in 1971.

A large mansion called Witham Place was situated behind the Tudor brick wall just past Spring Lodge. It was built about 1550 and was eventually demolished by the mill owner in 1850. This postcard view, postdated 1911, shows the road down to the mill, Spring Lodge and the grounds where Witham Place once stood.

This photograph shows some outbuildings which once stood by the mill house. The mill burned down in 1775, and again in 1882, but was not rebuilt the second time.

Spring Lodge was built by Robert Bretnall, the miller, in 1830 for himself and his family. A hundred years later this view is looking from the cabbage field on which Saxon Drive and Tithe Close now stand.

Until its destruction by fire, the mill stood immediately next to the house. The brick arches where the water left the wheels can still be seen from the road. Bretnall was a very prosperous miller and his flour was taken by wagon as far away as Colchester.

St Nicolas' Church was built, probably in the 1330s, of flint quarried from a gravel pit in Church Street and interspersed with Roman brick. The church has changed very little over the centuries as this turn-of-the-century postcard shows.

The Brandt Gimson wedding at St Nicolas' Church in October 1917. Baptisms, marriages and births are recorded from the seventeenth century. The churchyard has probably been used for burials for a thousand years.

Mr and Mrs Willshire lived in the
cottages by the church for a
number of years before the war.
This photograph of the couple was
taken at the side of the building in
1932.

The cottages date from the fifteenth century and were converted into three dwellings for
many years. This picture shows the younger Mr Willshire on his BSA in 1928. The
cottages have now been refurbished and converted back into one dwelling.

The old vicarage was a twenty-one room house built by Jonas Warley between 1680 and 1710. The grounds were landscaped by Philip Southcote of Witham Place about 1740, and the building encased in a brick façade. The house was reduced in size in the 1930s, but this photograph shows its previous glory.

Church Street was the old road to Cressing. This photograph features Frederick Hasler's grocery and general store which he ran from 1910 to about 1930. This scene is generally unchanged today.

Another view of Church Street, with No. 11, a fine Georgian house opposite Chalks Road, seen on the left.

The main terrace of cottages on the left was once the parish workhouse, known as Union House. It ceased to be a workhouse in 1839 when a new one (now Bridge Hospital) was opened in Hatfield Road. This view from the churchyard is dated 1908.

The same cottages from the Chipping Hill end. The brick house in the foreground was a Church of England infants school known as St Christopher's until it was closed in 1900. This photograph was taken when it was a furniture dealers, between 1914 and 1927. The house on the extreme right was demolished in the 1960s to make way for new shops.

This narrow stretch of Braintree Road was bypassed by Bellfield Road in 1971. Cullens Seeds warehouse is on the left.

# SECTION FIVE

# And District . . . the Surrounding Villages

Hatfield Peverel post office in about 1920. The Methodist church is in the background.

This unusual house, pictured in the 1920s, is believed to have been in Maldon Road, Hatfield Peverel.

The Green, Maldon Road, Hatfield Peverel, pictured after the First World War.

Another view of the Green, Hatfield Peverel, probably earlier and this time with a group of children posing for the camera.

The Street, Wickham Bishops, earlier this century.

This row of cottages, photographed around 1920, is believed to have been in Kelvedon Road, Wickham Bishops.

The old war memorial, Wickham Bishops, soon after the First World War. The view is largely unchanged today.

The old school, Wickham Bishops, in the 1920s. It is now used as a public library.

The rectory of St Bartholomew, Wickham Bishops, with the family outside. This card is dated 1915, but the picture would appear to be around the turn of the century.

The redundant and derelict St Peter's Church, Wickham Bishops, around 1920. It was leased to the 'Friends of Friendless Churches' in 1975.

Snow's Corner, Wickham Bishops, about 1913. Although it has had many changes of occupier, the building is still a general store.

Looking towards Tiptree from Snow's Corner early this century. The buildings are still there today.

Wickham Bishops station probably in the late 1890s. It was a typical country station with goods sidings and a station house. The house is still there but little else.

The branch line from Witham to Maldon opened on 2 October 1848 and closed for passengers on 6 September 1964 and completely in 1966. A rare feature of the line was a timber trestle bridge over the River Blackwater just outside Wickham Bishops. Although unused this structure is listed and is still intact.

Church Green, Terling, opposite the church. Little has changed since the photograph was taken before 1905.

The top of Oak Hill, Terling, looking eastward. This Spalding postcard dates from soon after 1900, and the foreground has since been built over. Viner Cottages are on the left and Garrets Mead on the right.

The Rayleigh Arms (known locally as the 'Monkey') is on the right of another Spalding postcard of about the same period. The small surgery is in the distance.

Gambles Green, Terling, looking northwards before 1913. It has since had several additions to the houses and two new homes built.

This Tudor house on Church Green, Terling, was once the offices for Lord Rayleigh's estate. This view dates from before 1905.

The east side of Hull Lane, Terling, before 1905. The house has disappeared, but new homes have been built all along the right-hand side, and living quarters added to the mill.

The windmill, Mill Lane, Terling. It is still occupied and used as a home, but the sails have been missing for many years.

The Rivenhall Oak in 1904. Although the tree remains, the buildings have all disappeared.

The Fox at Rivenhall End in 1904. This staggered junction on the London to Colchester trunk road has long since been widened and the public house rebuilt much further back.

Rivenhall Place has changed little outwardly since this 1925 picture.

These fishermen, pictured spearing eels in the lake in front of Rivenhall Place in 1917, caught 30 lbs on their first day.

The old rectory at Faulkbourne, about 1920.

The class outside Faulkbourne School, about 1920. The schoolmistress was known as 'Old Lady Beardwell'.

Apart from the road surface, this 1905 view of White Notley from the Witham side has hardly changed.

White Notley from the Cross Keys forecourt, about 1906. The little cottage between the main buildings was later demolished.

A charming view of St Etheldreda's Church, White Notley, in the early 1930s.

An early aerial view of Silver End garden village; the foundation stone of the first house was laid in April 1926.

Crittalls factory at Silver End after the Second World War.

The tool room inside the Crittalls factory in the 1950s.

Part of 'C' Co., 7th Essex Home Guard outside Silver End village hall during the Second World War. Included in the company were Mr Dyer, Charlie Smith, Mr Poulter, Dr Hughes, Evan Jenkins, Don Graham and Ernie Edwards.

Mr and Mrs Macdonald Graham outside their new home in Silver Street, Silver End, in 1935.

An electrical fault caused this catastrophic fire at the Co-operative Society departmental store in Silver End in 1951. A man in the tea-shop raised the alarm.

Mr and Mrs Sutton with their eleven children outside their thatched cottage in Temple Lane, Silver End, in 1918. Arthur (second from the left at the back) became a Co-op milkman and lived in a council house in Silver End from 1928 until his death in the 1980s.

# Acknowledgements

This book has been prepared under the auspices of the Witham and Countryside Society, and I should first like to acknowledge the help and support of the Society and its members during the course of the book's preparation. Particular thanks must go to John Page whose energetic support was essential in collecting and returning photographic collections. It would have been a monumental task without his help.

Lester Shelley's substantial collection has been the foundation of the book, while the Maurice Smith Witham History Collection, held by Witham Library and Howbridge School, and M.C. (Mick) Morarji's collection have also been invaluable. A full list of photographic contributors is given below:

L. Shelley • Maurice Smith Witham History Collection • M.C. Morarji
Braintree District Museum • Essex Police Museum • G. Capon • J. Mason
A. Scott • G.R. Mortimer • N. Bowdidge • C. Tay/lor • P. Church • R. Cullum
D. Dove • S. Gurton • J. Lock • E. Murdy • C. Simmonds • J. Simmonds
P. Slugocki • E. Strutt • P. Vojak • P. Wheaton • B. Young • P. Willshire

The principal sources for the introduction and captions were:

*Essex Headlines* by Stan Jarvis
*British Electorial Facts, 1832–1987* by F.W.S. Craig
*Essex at Work* by A.F.S. Brown
The many contributors to the Witham & Countryside Society's bulletin.
The Witham & Countryside Society's publications:
  *Guide to Newland Street*
  *Guide to Chipping Hill*

Grateful thanks are offered to all of them, and apologies tendered if any should inadvertently have been omitted.

# BRITAIN IN OLD PHOTOGRAPHS